Des Imagistes: An Anthology

Various Authors

Originally Published by
Albert and Charles Boni
1914

Contents

DES IMAGISTES	1
CHORICOS	3
TO A GREEK MARBLE	5
AU VIEUX JARDIN	7
LESBIA	9
BEAUTY THOU HAST HURT ME OVERMUCH	11
ARGYRIA	13
IN THE VIA SESTINA	15
THE RIVER	17
BROMIOS	19
TO ATTHIS *(After the Manuscript of Sappho now in Berlin)*	21
SITALKAS	23
HERMES OF THE WAYS	25
PRIAPUS *Keeper-of-Orchards*	27
ACON *(After Joannes Baptista Amaltheus)*	29
HERMONAX	31
EPIGRAM *(After the Greek)*	33
I	35

II	37
III	39
IV	41
V	43
NOCTURNES	45
IN A GARDEN	47
POSTLUDE	49
I HEAR AN ARMY	51
ΔΩRIA	53
THE RETURN	55
AFTER CH'U YUAN	57
LIU CH'E	59
FAN-PIECE FOR HER IMPERIAL LORD	61
TS'AI CHI'H	63
IN THE LITTLE OLD MARKET-PLACE *(To the Memory of A. V.)*	65
SCENTED LEAVES FROM A CHINESE JAR	67
THE BITTER PURPLE WILLOWS	67
THE GOLD FISH	67
THE INTOXICATED POET	67
THE JONQUILS	67
THE MERMAID	67
THE MIDDLE KINGDOM	68
THE MILKY WAY	68
THE SEA-SHELL	68
THE SWALLOW TOWER	68
THE ROSE	69
TO HULME (T. E.) AND FITZGERALD	71
VATES, THE SOCIAL REFORMER	73

FRAGMENTS ADDRESSED BY CLEARCHUS H. TO ALDI 75
    II   II . 43 75
    Pôetrie Prike phiphteen kenx   p. 43 75
    Poetry Price fifteen cents   p. 43 76

BIBLIOGRAPHY 77

DES IMAGISTES

«Κ   Σ ,   Α   ,   Δ .» E   B
"And she also was of Sikilia and was gay in the valleys of Ætna, and knew the Doric singing."

Richard Aldington Choricos   7 To a Greek Marble   10 Au Vieux Jardin   11 Lesbia   12 Beauty Thou Hast Hurt Me Overmuch   13 Argyria   14 In the Via Sestina   15 The River   16 Bromios   17 To Atthis   19

H. D. Sitalkas   20 Hermes of the Ways I   21 Hermes of the Ways II   22 Priapus   24 Acon   26 Hermonax   28 Epigram   30

F. S. Flint I   31 II Hallucination   32 III   33 IV   34 V The Swan   35

Skipwith Cannéll Nocturnes   36

Amy Lowell In a Garden   38

William Carlos Williams Postlude   39

James Joyce I Hear an Army   40

Ezra Pound Δ   41 The Return   42 After Ch'u Yuan   43 Liu Ch'e   44 Fan-Piece for Her Imperial Lord   45 Ts'ai Chi'h   46

Ford Madox Hueffer In the Little Old Market-Place   47

Allen Upward Scented Leaves from a Chinese Jar   51

John Cournos after K. Tetmaier The Rose   54

Documents To Hulme (T. E.) and Fitzgerald   57 Vates, the Social Reformer   59 Fragments Addressed by Clearchus H. to Aldi   62

Bibliography   63

CHORICOS

The ancient songs Pass deathward mournfully.

Cold lips that sing no more, and withered wreaths, Regretful eyes, and drooping breasts and wings— Symbols of ancient songs Mournfully passing Down to the great white surges, Watched of none Save the frail sea-birds And the lithe pale girls, Daughters of Okeanus.

And the songs pass From the green land Which lies upon the waves as a leaf On the flowers of hyacinth; And they pass from the waters, The manifold winds and the dim moon, And they come, Silently winging through soft Kimmerian dusk, To the quiet level lands That she keeps for us all, That she wrought for us all for sleep In the silver days of the earth's dawning— Proserpina, daughter of Zeus.

And we turn from the Kuprian's breasts, And we turn from thee, Phoibos Apollon, And we turn from the music of old And the hills that we loved and the meads, And we turn from the fiery day, And the lips that were over sweet; For silently Brushing the fields with red-shod feet, With purple robe Searing the flowers as with a sudden flame, Death, Thou hast come upon us.

And of all the ancient songs Passing to the swallow-blue halls By the dark streams of Persephone, This only remains: That we turn to thee, Death, That we turn to thee, singing One last song.

O Death, Thou art an healing wind That blowest over white flowers A-tremble with dew; Thou art a wind flowing Over dark leagues of lonely sea; Thou art the dusk and the fragrance; Thou art the lips of love mournfully smiling; Thou art the pale peace of one Satiate with old desires; Thou art the silence of beauty, And we look no more for the morning We yearn no more for the sun, Since with thy white hands, Death, Thou crownest us with the pallid chaplets, The slim colourless poppies Which in thy garden alone Softly thou gatherest.

And silently, And with slow feet approaching, And with bowed head and unlit eyes, We kneel before thee: And thou, leaning towards us, Caressingly layest upon us Flowers from thy thin cold hands, And, smiling as a chaste woman Knowing love in her heart, Thou sealest our eyes And the illimitable quietude Comes gently upon us.

Richard Aldington

TO A GREEK MARBLE

Π , White grave goddess, Pity my sadness, O silence of Paros.

I am not of these about thy feet, These garments and decorum; I am thy brother, Thy lover of aforetime crying to thee, And thou hearest me not.

I have whispered thee in thy solitudes Of our loves in Phrygia, The far ecstasy of burning noons When the fragile pipes Ceased in the cypress shade, And the brown fingers of the shepherd Moved over slim shoulders; And only the cicada sang.

I have told thee of the hills And the lisp of reeds And the sun upon thy breasts,

And thou hearest me not, Π , , Thou hearest me not.

Richard Aldington

AU VIEUX JARDIN

I have sat here happy in the gardens, Watching the still pool and the reeds And the dark clouds Which the wind of the upper air Tore like the green leafy boughs Of the divers-hued trees of late summer; But though I greatly delight In these and the water lilies, That which sets me nighest to weeping Is the rose and white colour of the smooth flag-stones, And the pale yellow grasses Among them.
   Richard Aldington

LESBIA

Use no more speech now; Let the silence spread gold hair above us Fold on delicate fold; You had the ivory of my life to carve. Use no more speech.
.   .   .   .
And Picus of Mirandola is dead; And all the gods they dreamed and fabled of, Hermes, and Thoth, and Christ, are rotten now, Rotten and dank.
.   .   .   .
And through it all I see your pale Greek face; Tenderness makes me as eager as a little child To love you

You morsel left half cold on Caesar's plate.

Richard Aldington

BEAUTY THOU HAST HURT ME OVERMUCH

The light is a wound to me. The soft notes Feed upon the wound.

Where wert thou born O thou woe That consumest my life? Whither comest thou?

Toothed wind of the seas, No man knows thy beginning. As a bird with strong claws Thou woundest me, O beautiful sorrow.

Richard Aldington

ARGYRIA

O you, O you most fair, Swayer of reeds, whisperer Among the flowering rushes, You have hidden your hands Beneath the poplar leaves, You have given them to the white waters.

Swallow-fleet, Sea-child cold from waves, Slight reed that sang so blithely in the wind, White cloud the white sun kissed into the air; Pan mourns for you.

White limbs, white song, Pan mourns for you.
Richard Aldington

IN THE VIA SESTINA

O daughter of Isis, Thou standest beside the wet highway Of this decayed Rome, A manifest harlot.

Straight and slim art thou As a marble phallus; Thy face is the face of Isis Carven

As she is carven in basalt. And my heart stops with awe At the presence of the gods,

There beside thee on the stall of images Is the head of Osiris Thy lord.

Richard Aldington

THE RIVER

I

I drifted along the river Until I moored my boat By these crossed trunks.

Here the mist moves Over fragile leaves and rushes, Colourless waters and brown fading hills.

She has come from beneath the trees, Moving within the mist, A floating leaf.

II

O blue flower of the evening, You have touched my face With your leaves of silver.

Love me for I must depart.

Richard Aldington

BROMIOS

The withered bonds are broken. The waxed reeds and the double pipe Clamour about me; The hot wind swirls Through the red pine trunks.

Io! the fauns and the satyrs. The touch of their shagged curled fur And blunt horns!

They have wine in heavy craters Painted black and red; Wine to splash on her white body. Io! She shrinks from the cold shower— Afraid, afraid!

Let the Maenads break through the myrtles And the boughs of the rohododaphnai. Let them tear the quick deers' flesh. Ah, the cruel, exquisite fingers!

Io! I have brought you the brown clusters, The ivy-boughs and pine-cones.

Your breasts are cold sea-ripples, But they smell of the warm grasses.

Throw wide the chiton and the peplum, Maidens of the Dew. Beautiful are your bodies, O Maenads, Beautiful the sudden folds, The vanishing curves of the white linen About you.

Io! Hear the rich laughter of the forest, The cymbals, The trampling of the panisks and the centaurs.

Richard Aldington.

TO ATTHIS (*After the Manuscript of Sappho now in Berlin*)

Atthis, far from me and dear Mnasidika, Dwells in Sardis; Many times she was near us So that we lived life well Like the far-famed goddess Whom above all things music delighted.

And now she is first among the Lydian women As the mighty sun, the rose-fingered moon, Beside the great stars.

And the light fades from the bitter sea And in like manner from the rich-blossoming earth; And the dew is shed upon the flowers, Rose and soft meadow-sweet And many-coloured melilote.

Many things told are remembered of sterile Atthis.

I yearn to behold thy delicate soul To satiate my desire. . . .
. . . .

Richard Aldington

SITALKAS

Thou art come at length More beautiful Than any cool god In a chamber under Lycia's far coast, Than any high god Who touches us not Here in the seeded grass. Aye, than Argestes Scattering the broken leaves.
    H. D.

HERMES OF THE WAYS

I

The hard sand breaks, And the grains of it Are clear as wine.

Far off over the leagues of it, The wind, Playing on the wide shore, Piles little ridges, And the great waves Break over it.

But more than the many-foamed ways Of the sea, I know him Of the triple path-ways, Hermes, Who awaiteth.

Dubious, Facing three ways, Welcoming wayfarers, He whom the sea-orchard Shelters from the west, From the east Weathers sea-wind; Fronts the great dunes.

Wind rushes Over the dunes, And the coarse, salt-crusted grass Answers.

Heu, It whips round my ankles!

II

Small is This white stream, Flowing below ground From the poplar-shaded hill, But the water is sweet.

Apples on the small trees Are hard, Too small, Too late ripened By a desperate sun That struggles through sea-mist.

The boughs of the trees Are twisted By many bafflings; Twisted are The small-leafed boughs. But the shadow of them Is not the shadow of the mast head Nor of the torn sails.

Hermes, Hermes, The great sea foamed, Gnashed its teeth about me; But you have waited, Where sea-grass tangles with Shore-grass.

H. D.

PRIAPUS
Keeper-of-Orchards

I saw the first pear As it fell. The honey-seeking, golden-banded, The yellow swarm Was not more fleet than I, (Spare us from loveliness!) And I fell prostrate, Crying, Thou hast flayed us with thy blossoms; Spare us the beauty Of fruit-trees!

The honey-seeking Paused not, The air thundered their song, And I alone was prostrate.

O rough-hewn God of the orchard, I bring thee an offering; Do thou, alone unbeautiful (Son of the god), Spare us from loveliness.

The fallen hazel-nuts, Stripped late of their green sheaths, The grapes, red-purple, Their berries Dripping with wine, Pomegranates already broken, And shrunken fig, And quinces untouched, I bring thee as offering.

H. D.

ACON (*After Joannes Baptista Amaltheus*)

I

Bear me to Dictaeus, And to the steep slopes; To the river Erymanthus.

I choose spray of dittany, Cyperum frail of flower, Buds of myrrh, All-healing herbs, Close pressed in calathes.

For she lies panting, Drawing sharp breath, Broken with harsh sobs, She, Hyella, Whom no god pitieth.

II

Dryads, Haunting the groves, Nereids, Who dwell in wet caves, For all the whitish leaves of olive-branch, And early roses, And ivy wreathes, woven gold berries, Which she once brought to your altars, Bear now ripe fruits from Arcadia, And Assyrian wine To shatter her fever.

The light of her face falls from its flower, As a hyacinth, Hidden in a far valley, Perishes upon burnt grass.

Pales, Bring gifts, Bring your Phoenician stuffs, And do you, fleet-footed nymphs, Bring offerings, Illyrian iris, And a branch of shrub, And frail-headed poppies.

H. D.

HERMONAX

Gods of the sea; Ino, Leaving warm meads For the green, grey-green fastnesses Of the great deeps; And Palemon, Bright striker of sea-shaft, Hear me.

Let all whom the sea loveth, Come to its altar front, And I Who can offer no other sacrifice to thee Bring this.

Broken by great waves, The wavelets flung it here, This sea-gliding creature, This strange creature like a weed, Covered with salt foam, Torn from the hillocks Of rock.

I, Hermonax, Caster of nets, Risking chance, Plying the sea craft, Came on it.

Thus to sea god Cometh gift of sea wrack; I, Hermonax, offer it To thee, Ino, And to Palemon.

H. D.

EPIGRAM (*After the Greek*)

The golden one is gone from the banquets; She, beloved of Atimetus, The swallow, the bright Homonoea: Gone the dear chatterer.
   H. D.

I

London, my beautiful, it is not the sunset nor the pale green sky shimmering through the curtain of the silver birch, nor the quietness; it is not the hopping of birds upon the lawn, nor the darkness stealing over all things that moves me.

But as the moon creeps slowly over the tree-tops among the stars, I think of her and the glow her passing sheds on men.

London, my beautiful, I will climb into the branches to the moonlit tree-tops, that my blood may be cooled by the wind.

F. S. Flint

II

I know this room, and there are corridors: the pictures, I have seen before; the statues and those gems in cases I have wandered by before,— stood there silent and lonely in a dream of years ago.

I know the dark of night is all around me; my eyes are closed, and I am half asleep. My wife breathes gently at my side.

But once again this old dream is within me, and I am on the threshold waiting, wondering, pleased, and fearful. Where do those doors lead, what rooms lie beyond them? I venture. . . .

But my baby moves and tosses from side to side, and her need calls me to her.

Now I stand awake, unseeing, in the dark, and I move towards her cot. . . . I shall not reach her . . . There is no direction. . . . I shall walk on. . . .

    F. S. Flint

III

Immortal? . . . No, they cannot be, these people, nor I.

Tired faces, eyes that have never seen the world, bodies that have never lived in air, lips that have never minted speech, they are the clipped and garbled, blocking the highway. They swarm and eddy between the banks of glowing shops towards the red meat, the potherbs, the cheapjacks, or surge in before the swift rush of the clanging trams,— pitiful, ugly, mean, encumbering.

Immortal? . . . In a wood, watching the shadow of a bird leap from frond to frond of bracken, I am immortal.

But these?

F. S. Flint

IV

The grass is beneath my head; and I gaze at the thronging stars in the night.
 They fall . . . they fall. . . . I am overwhelmed, and afraid.
 Each leaf of the aspen is caressed by the wind, and each is crying.
 And the perfume of invisible roses deepens the anguish.
 Let a strong mesh of roots feed the crimson of roses upon my heart; and then fold over the hollow where all the pain was.
 F. S. Flint

V

Under the lily shadow and the gold and the blue and mauve that the whin and the lilac pour down on the water, the fishes quiver.

Over the green cold leaves and the rippled silver and the tarnished copper of its neck and beak, toward the deep black water beneath the arches, the swan floats slowly.

Into the dark of the arch the swan floats and into the black depth of my sorrow it bears a white rose of flame.

F. S. Flint

NOCTURNES

I

Thy feet, That are like little, silver birds, Thou hast set upon pleasant ways; Therefore I will follow thee, Thou Dove of the Golden Eyes, Upon any path will I follow thee, For the light of thy beauty Shines before me like a torch.

II

Thy feet are white Upon the foam of the sea; Hold me fast, thou bright Swan, Lest I stumble, And into deep waters.

III

Long have I been But the Singer beneath thy Casement, And now I am weary. I am sick with longing, O my Belovéd; Therefore bear me with thee Swiftly Upon our road.

IV

With the net of thy hair Thou hast fished in the sea, And a strange fish Hast thou caught in thy net; For thy hair, Belovéd, Holdeth my heart Within its web of gold.

V

I am weary with love, and thy lips Are night-born poppies. Give me therefore thy lips That I may know sleep.

VI

I am weary with longing, I am faint with love; For upon my head has the moonlight Fallen As a sword.

Skipwith Cannéll

IN A GARDEN

Gushing from the mouths of stone men To spread at ease under the sky In granite-lipped basins, Where iris dabble their feet And rustle to a passing wind, The water fills the garden with its rushing, In the midst of the quiet of close-clipped lawns.

Damp smell the ferns in tunnels of stone, Where trickle and plash the fountains, Marble fountains, yellowed with much water.

Splashing down moss-tarnished steps It falls, the water; And the air is throbbing with it; With its gurgling and running; With its leaping, and deep, cool murmur.

And I wished for night and you. I wanted to see you in the swimming-pool, White and shining in the silver-flecked water. While the moon rode over the garden, High in the arch of night, And the scent of the lilacs was heavy with stillness.

Night and the water, and you in your whiteness, bathing!

Amy Lowell

POSTLUDE

Now that I have cooled to you Let there be gold of tarnished masonry, Temples soothed by the sun to ruin That sleep utterly. Give me hand for the dances, Ripples at Philæ, in and out, And lips, my Lesbian, Wall flowers that once were flame.

Your hair is my Carthage And my arms the bow And our words arrows To shoot the stars, Who from that misty sea Swarm to destroy us. But you're there beside me Oh, how shall I defy you Who wound me in the night With breasts shining Like Venus and like Mars? The night that is shouting Jason When the loud eaves rattle As with waves above me Blue at the prow of my desire! O prayers in the dark! O incense to Poseidon! Calm in Atlantis.

William Carlos Williams

I HEAR AN ARMY

I hear an army charging upon the land, And the thunder of horses plunging; foam about their knees: Arrogant, in black armour, behind them stand, Disdaining the rains, with fluttering whips, the Charioteers.

They cry into the night their battle name: I moan in sleep when I hear afar their whirling laughter. They cleave the gloom of dreams, a blinding flame, Clanging, clanging upon the heart as upon an anvil.

They come shaking in triumph their long grey hair: They come out of the sea and run shouting by the shore. My heart, have you no wisdom thus to despair? My love, my love, my love, why have you left me alone?

James Joyce

ΔΩΡΙΑ

Be in me as the eternal moods of the bleak wind, and not As transient things are— gaiety of flowers. Have me in the strong loneliness of sunless cliffs And of grey waters. Let the gods speak softly of us In days hereafter, The shadowy flowers of Orcus Remember Thee.
    Ezra Pound

THE RETURN

See, they return; ah, see the tentative Movements, and the slow feet, The trouble in the pace and the uncertain Wavering!

See, they return, one, and by one, With fear, as half-awakened; As if the snow should hesitate And murmur in the wind and half turn back; These were the "Wing'd-with-Awe," Inviolable.

Gods of the winged shoe! With them the silver hounds sniffing the trace of air! Haie! Haie! These were the swift to harry; These the keen-scented; These were the souls of blood.

Slow on the leash, pallid the leash-men!

Ezra Pound

AFTER CH'U YUAN

I will get me to the wood Where the gods walk garlanded in wisteria, By the silver-blue flood move others with ivory cars. There come forth many maidens to gather grapes for the leopards, my friend. For there are leopards drawing the cars.

I will walk in the glade, I will come out of the new thicket and accost the procession of maidens.

Ezra Pound

LIU CH'E

The rustling of the silk is discontinued, Dust drifts over the courtyard, There is no sound of footfall, and the leaves Scurry into heaps and lie still, And she the rejoicer of the heart is beneath them:
A wet leaf that clings to the threshold.
Ezra Pound.

FAN-PIECE FOR HER IMPERIAL LORD

O fan of white silk, clear as frost on the grass-blade, You also are laid aside.
 Ezra Pound

TS'AI CHI'H

The petals fall in the fountain, the orange coloured rose-leaves, Their ochre clings to the stone. Ezra Pound.

IN THE LITTLE OLD MARKET-PLACE *(To the Memory of A. V.)*

It rains, it rains, From gutters and drains And gargoyles and gables: It drips from the tables That tell us the tolls upon grains, Oxen, asses, sheep, turkeys and fowls Set into the rain-soaked wall Of the old Town Hall.

The mountains being so tall And forcing the town on the river, The market's so small That, with the wet cobbles, dark arches and all, The owls (For in dark rainy weather the owls fly out Well before four), so the owls In the gloom Have too little room And brush by the saint on the fountain In veering about.

The poor saint on the fountain! Supported by plaques of the giver To whom we're beholden; His name was de Sales And his wife's name von Mangel.

(Now is he a saint or archangel?) He stands on a dragon On a ball, on a column Gazing up at the vines on the mountain: And his falchion is golden And his wings are all golden. He bears golden scales And in spite of the coils of his dragon, without hint of alarm or invective Looks up at the mists on the mountain.

(Now what saint or archangel Stands winged on a dragon, Bearing golden scales and a broad bladed sword all golden? Alas, my knowledge Of all the saints of the college, Of all these glimmering, olden Sacred and misty stories Of angels and saints and old glories . . . Is sadly defective.) The poor saint on the fountain . . .

On top of his column Gazes up sad and solemn. But is it towards the top of the mountain Where the spindrifty haze is That he gazes? Or is it into the casement Where the girl sits sewing? There's no knowing.

Hear it rain! And from eight leaden pipes in the ball he stands on That has eight leaden and copper bands on, There gurgle and drain Eight driblets of water down into the basin.

And he stands on his dragon And the girl sits sewing High, very high in her casement And before her are many geraniums in a parket All growing and blowing In box upon box From the gables right down to the basement With frescoes and carvings and paint . . .

The poor saint! It rains and it rains, In the market there isn't an ox, And in all the emplacement For waggons there isn't a waggon, Not a stall for a grape or a raisin, Not a soul in the market Save the saint on his dragon With the rain dribbling down in the basin, And the maiden that sews in the casement.

They are still and alone, *Mutterseelens* alone, And the rain dribbles down from his heels and his crown, From wet stone to wet stone. It's grey as at dawn, And the owls, grey and fawn, Call from the little town hall With its arch in the wall, Where the fire-hooks are stored.

From behind the flowers of her casement That's all gay with the carvings and paint, The maiden gives a great yawn, But the poor saint— No doubt he's as bored! Stands still on his column Uplifting his sword With never the ease of a yawn From wet dawn to wet dawn . . .

Ford Madox Hueffer

SCENTED LEAVES FROM A CHINESE JAR

THE BITTER PURPLE WILLOWS

Meditating on the glory of illustrious lineage I lifted up my eyes and beheld the bitter purple willows growing round the tombs of the exalted Mings.

THE GOLD FISH

Like a breath from hoarded musk, Like the golden fins that move Where the tank's green shadows part— Living flames out of the dusk— Are the lightning throbs of love In the passionate lover's heart.

THE INTOXICATED POET

A poet, having taken the bridle off his tongue, spoke thus: "More fragrant than the heliotrope, which blooms all the year round, better than vermilion letters on tablets of sendal, are thy kisses, thou shy one!"

THE JONQUILS

I have heard that a certain princess, when she found that she had been married by a demon, wove a wreath of jonquils and sent it to the lover of former days.

THE MERMAID

The sailor boy who leant over the side of the Junk of Many Pearls, and combed the green tresses of the sea with his ivory fingers, believing that he had heard the voice of a mermaid, cast his body down between the waves.

THE MIDDLE KINGDOM

The emperors of fourteen dynasties, clad in robes of yellow silk embroidered with the Dragon, wearing gold diadems set with pearls and rubies, and seated on thrones of incomparable ivory, have ruled over the Middle Kingdom for four thousand years.

THE MILKY WAY

My mother taught me that every night a procession of junks carrying lanterns moves silently across the sky, and the water sprinkled from their paddles falls to the earth in the form of dew. I no longer believe that the stars are junks carrying lanterns, no longer that the dew is shaken from their oars.

THE SEA-SHELL

To the passionate lover, whose sighs come back to him on every breeze, all the world is like a murmuring sea-shell.

THE SWALLOW TOWER

Amid a landscape flickering with poplars, and netted by a silver stream, the Swallow Tower stands in the haunts of the sun. The winds out of the four quarters of heaven come to sigh around it, the clouds forsake the zenith to bathe it with continuous kisses. Against its sun-worn walls a sea of orchards breaks in white foam; and from the battlements the birds that flit below are seen like fishes in a green moat. The windows of the Tower stand open day and night; the winged Guests come when they please, and hold communication with the unknown Keeper of the Tower.

    Allen Upward

THE ROSE

I remember a day when I stood on the sea shore at Nice, holding a scarlet rose in my hands.

The calm sea, caressed by the sun, was brightly garmented in blue, veiled in gold, and violet, verging on silver.

Gently the waves lapped the shore, and scattering into pearls, emeralds and opals, hastened towards my feet with a monotonous, rhythmical sound, like the prolonged note of a single harp-string.

High in the clear, blue-golden sky hung the great, burning disc of the sun.

White seagulls hovered above the waves, now barely touching them with their snow-white breasts, now rising anew into the heights, like butterflies over the green meadows . . .

Far in the east, a ship, trailing its smoke, glided slowly from sight as though it had foundered in the waste.

I threw the rose into the sea, and watched it, caught in the wave, receding, red on the snow-white foam, paler on the emerald wave.

And the sea continued to return it to me, again and again, at last no longer a flower, but strewn petals on restless water.

So with the heart, and with all proud things. In the end nothing remains but a handful of petals of what was once a proud flower . . .

John Cournos after K. Tetmaier

TO HULME (T. E.) AND FITZGERALD

Is there for feckless poverty That grins at ye for a' that! A hired slave to none am I, But under-fed for a' that; For a' that and a' that, The toils I shun and a' that, My name but mocks the guinea stamp, And Pound's dead broke for a' that.

Although my linen still is clean, My socks fine silk and a' that, Although I dine and drink good wine— Say, twice a week, and a' that; For a' that and a' that, My tinsel shows and a' that, These breeks 'll no last many weeks 'Gainst wear and tear and a' that.

Ye see this birkie ca'ed a bard, Wi' cryptic eyes and a' that, Aesthetic phrases by the yard; It's but E. P. for a' that, For a' that and a' that, My verses, books and a' that, The man of independent means He looks and laughs at a' that.

One man will make a novelette And sell the same and a' that. For verse nae man can siller get, Nae editor maun fa' that. For a' that and a' that, Their royalties and a' that, Wib time to loaf and will to write I'll stick to rhyme for a' that.

And ye may prise and gang your ways Wi' pity, sneers and a' that, I know my trade and God has made Some men to rhyme and a' that, For a' that and a' that, I maun gang on for a' that Wi' verse to verse until the hearse Carts off me wame and a' that.

WRITTEN FOR THE CENACLE OF 1909 VIDE INTRODUCTION TO "THE COMPLETE POETICAL WORKS OF T. E. HULME," PUBLISHED AT THE END OF "RIPOSTES."

VATES, THE SOCIAL REFORMER

What shall be said of him, this cock-o'-hoop? (I'm just a trifle bored, dear God of mine, Dear unknown God, dear chicken-pox of Heaven, I'm bored I say), But still—my social friend— (One has to be familiar in one's discourse) While he was puffing out his jets of wit Over his swollen-bellied pipe, one thinks, One thinks, you know, of quite a lot of things.

(Dear unknown God, dear, queer-faced God, Queer, queer, queer, queer-faced God, You blanky God, be quiet for half minute, And when I've shut up Rates, and sat on Naboth, I'll tell you half a dozen things or so.)

There goes a flock of starlings— Now half a dozen years ago, (Shut up, you blighted God, and let me speak) I should have hove my sporting air-gun up And blazed away—and now I let 'em go— It's odd how one changes; Yes, that's High Germany.

But still, when he was smiling like a Chinese queen, Looking as queer (I do assure you, God) As any Chinese queen I ever saw; And tiddle-whiddle-whiddling about prose, Trying to quiz a mutton-headed poetaster, And choking all the time with politics— Why then I say, I contemplated him And marveled (God! I marveled, Write it in prose, dear God. Yes, in red ink.) And marveled, as I said, At the stupendous quantity of mind And the amazing quality thereof.

Dear God of mine, It's really most amazing, doncherknow, But really, God, I *can't* get off the mark; Look here, you queer-faced God, This fellow makes me sick with all his talk, His ha'penny gibes at Celtic bards And followers of Dante—honest folk!— Because, dear God, the rotten beggar goes And makes a Chinese blue-stocking From half-digested dreams of Munich-air. And then— God, why should I write it down?— But Rates and Naboth Aren't half such silly fools as he is (God) For they are frankly asinine, While he pretends to sanity, Modernity, (dear God, dear God).

It's bad enough, dear God of mine, That you have set me down in London town, Endowed me with a tattered velvet coat, Soft collar and black hat and Greek ambitions; You might have left me there.

But now you send This "vates" here, this sage social reformer (Yes, God, you rotten Roman Catholic) To put his hypothetical conceptions Of what a poor young poetaster would think Into his own damned shape, and then to attack it To his own great contemplative satisfaction. What have I done, O God, That so much bitterness should flop on me? Social Reformer! That's the beggar's name. He'd have me write bad novels like himself.

Yes, God, I know it's after closing time; And yes, I know I've smoked his cigarettes; But watch that sparrow on the fountain in the rain. How half a dozen years ago, (Shut up, you blighted God, and let me speak) I should have hove my sporting air-gun up And blazed away—and now I let him go— It's odd how one changes; Yes, that's High Germany.

R. A.

FRAGMENTS ADDRESSED BY CLEARCHUS H. TO ALDI

Π   Π   . 43

                    (,   ) (1)   H
                                        (   ) (2)
       ,   (,   ,   ) (3)
                    (K   ) (4)   ,

Notes. (1) A vehicle conducting passengers from Athens, the capital of Greece, to the temple of the winds, which stands in a respectable suburb. (2) Rendered by Butler, "O God! O Montreal!" (3) Sappho!!!!! (4) Xenophon's Anabasis. F. M. H.

Pôetrie Prike phiphteen kenx   p. 43

I haue sat here harrie in mi armchair (p tnêbus, p tnêbus) (1) uatching the still Êound and the kid uith the dark hair huich the uind oph mi upraised uoike tore like a green matted mess (Ô andres Athênaioi) (2) oph uet kobuebs and seaueed at tuiligt, but thoug I greatlie deligted (êraman men egô sethen, Aldi, palai pota) (3) in thêse and the Ezra huiskers that huich sets me nirest to ueeping (ho de Klearchos eipe) (4) is the klassikal rhythm oph the rare speeches, Ô the unspôken speeches Hellenik.

75

Poetry Price fifteen cents   p. 43

I have sat here Harry in my armchair (Putney-bus, Putney-bus) (1) watching the still hound and the kid with the dark hair which the wind of my upraised voice tore like a green matted mess (Ô andres Athênaioi) (2) of wet cobwebs and seaweed at twilight, but though I greatly delighted (êraman men egô sethen, Aldi, palai pota) (3) in these and the Ezra whiskers that which sets me nearest to weeping (ho de Klearchos eipe) (4) is the classical rhythm of the rare speeches, O the unspoken speeches Hellenic.

BIBLIOGRAPHY

F. S. Flint—"The Net of the Stars." Published by Elkin Mathews, 4 Cork St., London, W.

Ezra Pound—Collected Poems (Personae, Exultations, Canzoni, Ripostes). Published by Elkin Mathews.

TRANSLATIONS:

"The Sonnets and Ballate of Guido Cavalcanti." Published by Small, Maynard & Co., Boston.

The Canzoni of Arnaut Daniel. R. F. Seymour & Co., Fine Arts Bldg., Chicago.

PROSE:

"The Spirit of Romance." A study of mediaeval poetry. Dent & Sons. London.

Ford Madox Hueffer—"Collected Poems." Published by Max Goschen, 20 Gt. Russel St., London. Forty volumes of prose with various publishers.

Allen Upward—Author of "The New Word," "The Divine Mystery," etc., etc.

The "Scented Leaves" appears in "Poetry" for September 1913.

William Carlos Williams—"The Tempers." Published by Elkin Mathews.

Amy Lowell—"A Dome of Many Coloured Glass." Published by Houghton, Mifflin, Boston.

www.ingramcontent.com/pod-product-compliance
Ingram Content Group UK Ltd.
Pitfield, Milton Keynes, MK11 3LW, UK
UKHW020756150525
5932UKWH00019B/227